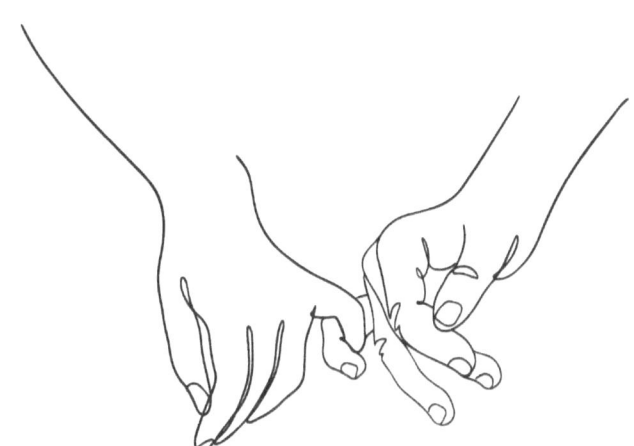

Copyright © 2021 by LaVan Robinson & Teresa James

Poetic Ecstasy

All rights reserved

No part of this publication may be reproduced or transmitted in any form or by any means electronic or mechanical, including photocopy, recording, or any information storage and retrieval system now known or invented, without permission in writing from the publisher, except by a reviewer who wishes to quote brief passages in connection with a review written for inclusion in a magazine, blog, or broadcast.

Paperback ISBN: 978-0-578-94464-7

www.TeresaJamesPoetry.com

Poetic Ecstasy

Stimulating the Heart and Soul

LaVan Robinson & Teresa James

Table of Contents

Cosmic……………………………………………………....7
A Poet……………………………………………………...9
I am a Poet……………………………………………….10
Rewind…………………………………………………...11
Dreams…………………………………………………..13
Torn……………………………………………………....15
Work and Succeed……………………………………....17
Principles………………………………………………..19
Love Haze……………………………………………….21
Cotton Candy………………………………………….....23
Climatic Top…………………………………………....25
Alive……………………………………………………..27
S'mores………………………………………………....29
Ice Cream……………………………………………....31
Together Forever Making………………………………33
Memories………………………………………………..35
Sure……………………………………………………...36
Self Imposed……………………………………………37
Beautification………………………………………….....39
Curiosity………..……………………………………….41
Tenderness……………………………………………...43
Happily Reside………………………………………….45
Keep Me Coming……………………………………….47
On Love's Foundations…………………………………48
Come True……………………………………………....49
Endlessly………………………………………………...51
Love Will Always Last………………………………….53

Love My Way..54
More Beautiful..55
Honey Nectar..59
Moon...61
In Tune..62
My Favorite Things...63
Shower Me...65
Enticing Grips...67
Natural Beauty..69
Do you want me?...70
Telepathy...71
Sleeping Beauty..73
Mastered..75
Dreams Are Made Of..77
Reside..79
The Love Game...81
Living, Breathing, and Being....................................83
The Busy Bee..85
Galactic Love..87

Dedicated to:

All the Lovers who complete one another.

Cosmic

If I was your twin flame
would you light my fire
to ignite the spark?

It would have
never
gone out.

An inferno when joined
to light up the dark.

Would you brand me deeply
and leave your mark?

A cosmic display so bright
leaving all vision stark.

The stars will dance
as we both are in a trance
of passion pressing towards
destiny as we take the stance.

Forever expanding love
filling all voids with
ecstasy and romance.

My confidant, lover, and friend
I will adore you to the end.

The universal red carpet
is set under the foundations of
our divine love.

A Poet

If my husband were a poet?

He'd write me a love letter
which no one else could see.
He'd scribble the lines and
words that meet our destiny.

He'd explore compositions
which I will never ignore.
He'd write intriguing words
that only I love and adore.

If my husband were a poet...
Every word would be music to my
ears drawing my inhibitions near;
knowing that we're the perfect pair.

He'd write his words in my heart
that only my ears could hear.
Every line would be a treasure
which means it brings me pleasure.

I am a Poet

I will write you within
a mystical garden of white roses.
Cleansing my soul with the purity
of your sweet aroma—
which manifests a renewal of self.

We will plant seeds of ecstasy,
slow grinds, cultivating wet dreams.
I am delighted and enlightened to
the fullest extent of pleasure.

The synchronization of our love making
will heighten awareness and awakening
into the unconscious freedom of expression.

I will write you among the heavenly alignment
and declare our love among the moon and stars.
I will write you in the essence of my being.

Rewind

If I could give you back time...
I would rewind to the places
where I lost trust in you which
subtly damaged my mind.

I would visit the walks in the park
to show you what broke us apart.
I would take strolls on the beach
and then reminisce about your
promises without a breach.

I would travel the dark roads
and let the stars guide me to the east.
Knowing that towards the end of
our journey brings us both peace.

These are the places where
I would go, that only love can know.
Let me rewind, so this time you
would always and forever be mine.

When I was sinking in hopelessness and despair,
you extended your branch of love
and I was spared.

Dreams

When I had you,
I had love at its very best.
I was wrong to treat you so badly
and now that part I so deeply regret.

You left and went away
and it also took the sunshine
out of my life and in my day.
I would give anything—
to have you back.

I'll even sell my soul to the devil,
and that's a fact...

Life hasn't been the same without you;
please come back,
and make this reunion between us come true.
I realize now...what I had in my life.

I was so wrong to let it slip
through my hands,
like grains of sands...

If it isn't meant to be again,
I'll heavily use my imagination
and make it reality
in my dreams.

Torn

Envision if I were to seduce your mind.
Integrity is what I'm searching to find.

Beneath the layers of resentment and fear.
Pulling my emotions you drew me near.

To find parts of you that I wish weren't true.
My love and passion I freely gave to you.

Little did I know it would be misconstrued.
Leaving me broken, sad and blue.

It never crossed my thoughts...
Nor something I knew you would do.

Where does it leave me today?
In a place where I can't stay.

To be free and live in peace,
is where my heart wants to be.

I gave you a promise of love through eternity.
Hoping, wishing and believing...

But instead you lied and hurt me.

Drifting on the sea of hopelessness,
your love shined like a beacon of hope.

Work and Succeed

Since you've been away...
My days and nights have been very cold and lonely.
I pray it's in the cards and we find our way to get back
together and make this love work and succeed.

You're a divine blessing, definitely one of a kind.
One glance into those mesmerizing eyes.
I start to lose my equilibrium and my mind.

I'm tired of sitting around daydreaming about how
I would do it so differently, if only I had the chance.
I love you still with all my heart and on that
I proclaim, I boldly stand.

I was a fool...
To take you for granted and your precious love.
Until the day you come back to me, I'll be praying
for you and thinking of us immensely.

Holding you in my arms tight, looking into your
beautiful eyes, and kissing you is what I'll do.
Forever we'll both be so happy but first we have
to find a way to make this love work and succeed.

Principles

Our love will shine brighter
than the sun, moon and the stars
that lights up the sky.

The powerful constellation
will be an enlightenment
to the spiritual, mental, and physical eye.

We will make love
on the mystic clouds of ecstasy.
Lightning will not be able to match its intensity.

The universe will be our playground
and the angels in heaven
will rejoice and sing.

Concerning the love—
which we have been blessed with;
indescribably so profound.

In your lair of satisfaction
and pleasure
is where I comfortably lay.

I'm your very happy partner,
to your lovin' and every command you say
without hesitation, I will obey.

We were destined for one another
from and after the manifestation of time.
Our hearts beat as one...

And I'm blessed to experience
a woman who is so unique,
special and so so kind.

Together there's nothing
we're not capable of—as long as we
always put first for each other.

And the principles of our strong,
amazing, phenomenal friendship...
and unconditional love.

Love Haze

The intensity
from the sweltering heat
of your powerful love—
to my soul and being
unleashes unadulterated,
steamy passions.

The thickness of ecstasy
resonates within my fantasies
and dreams...

Now happy are my earthly days
as I allow love
to brighten my way,
as I fall deeper
somewhat slightly dazed—
within the cycle of
the ultimate love haze.

My faith is once again renewed as I fall more and more in love with you.

Cotton Candy

You're sweeter than cotton candy
and for your tasty, sticky treat,
my body and sweet tooth
will be fully demanding.

One big taste of you
has my sugar and energy level
on extremely high.
Yum umm good are you
and what you definitely
bring into my life.

Sweetness that I never tasted
or experienced before.
Your love is so good and plenty—
leaves me skipping dinner,
straight to dessert.

Completely satisfied to my core
and so much more.
I'm so very delighted
to have your delectable treat.

Its healthy nutritional value
always makes me spiritually,
mentally and physically,
so happy and complete...
Providing all the sweetness in life
I ever want, desire and need.

Climatic Top

Every day is like the day
I first laid my eyes on you.
Before that day,
I was so very lonely...
constantly searching and looking
for my true one and only.

Now, just like that—
you suddenly appeared
and all of my worries were put to rest
and my tedious search for undying happiness
and Love was finally fulfilled.

You brought into my dreary and dark day
an ominous light that led
and showed me out of its grip.
I'm so blessed to have plenty of sunshine
in my Life and day.

I was always looking out for love
in some way or the other...
Now that you're here,
I'm all yours and will never love another.

Every time we kiss
and I touch your soft velvety skin,
I fall more helplessly in love with you—
over and over, again and again.

I don't want this Love and feeling to ever stop
because every chance we get,
we both together in unison...
reach the mountain peak.

It's pure stimulating enlightenment
of our whole essence and being—
drenching and satisfying climatic top.

Alive

Now that I have experienced your lovin'
I refuse to do without it in my world.
I need and want you so much, baby.
You have come and changed my frown
into a beautiful smile.

I yearn for your sweetness like breast milk
to a crying newborn child.
You make living again worth the while
and I'm mesmerized and captivated
by your beautiful essence
that makes me take a bow.

I'll honor you all the days I'm alive
and to make and keep you happy
is everyday I would strive for.
Your most inner desires,
I would please and your every wish
is my command as we experience candlelight
and slow, slow sensuous dance.

No matter what, I'll do anything
just to keep you satisfied...
I'll always and forever cherish the days,
seconds, minutes and hours—
we're both nestled in each other's arms
so very much alive.

We walk on the clouds of passions
as we're fulfilled in love's rhapsody
and satisfaction.

S'mores

You and I together
are what s'mores are made of.

Your tantalizing essence
makes my body erupt creamy delights
on top of your sweet tasty chocolate.

Its sensuous bakery delight is good
and arouses my taste buds.

When melted properly,
we manifest plentiful mountains
of chocolate swirls
in the mixture of our love.

In the oven of your heated passions,
we are delighted and enlightened
to bake from scratch—

Erotic and exotic treats
that stimulate the spiritual,
mental and physical expression
of our lovemaking.

Love is a repetitive motion that involves perfection of the emotions.

Ice Cream

As your ice cream slowly melts
on the cone of my existence.

In its essence and arousing sweetness,
I'm so delighted by its delicious treat.

My tongue willingly catches the stickiness—
as it drips from the validity of your pleasure box.

The powerful elixir stimulates the static
churning of eroticism to maximum strength.

I get very excited while deep within
the motion and potency...

Manifesting life and completing
the soul's insatiable exotic appetite
that magnifies our love's ominous light.

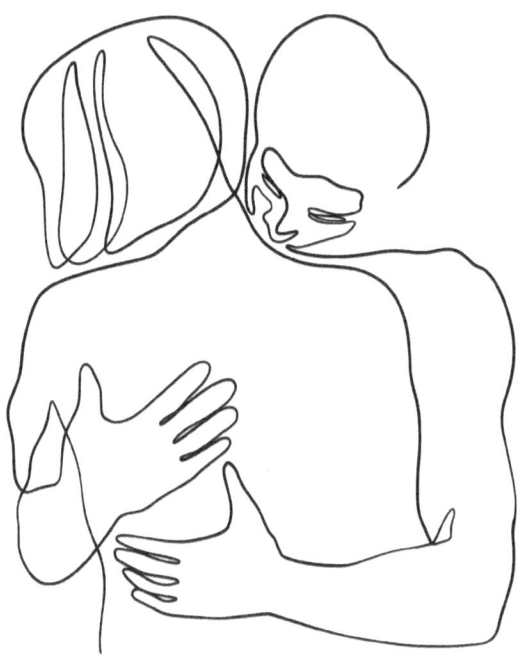

Together Forever Making

Situations will change
or get blown out of proportion
but as the days go on, girl,
I'll give you more love
and my utmost devotion...

I'll keep it always exciting
within this love ocean—
and love you down
with the slowest of motion.

I'll make it feel like something
out of an erotic dream
and in passions delight,
you'll let out small exotic screams.

In a thousand delights,
you'll be squirming
and uncontrollably shaking...

From the passionate artistry
that we'll be together,
forever making.

Out of the visions of my dreams and fantasy.
In my world— I paint your validity into reality.

Memories

Take a walk with me and let's
stroll down the road of memories
and let our emotions run like
raging cool waters of ecstasy.

Exploring the depths of each other's mind.
Reminiscing as we travel insatiably
through time.

Embracing one another,
as we combine the perimeters
which keeps us entwined.

Strolling down memory lane—
We'll stop and view the sights of
how this love became.

Was it the way you look or the way you
make me scream your name?

Holding me tight and quenching my thirst.
You're special because you were
my very first.

It captured us and we became willing
to its desires—grateful for this love on
a different trajectory took us so much higher.

Sure

Under the skies
of the solar eclipse
is where our lips met
for our very first kiss.

The amazement in both of our eyes
came as no surprise
in our pursuit as love's rhapsodies
slowly manifested—
into soulful heavenly visions
of bliss in our minds.

My essence and soul
was so blessed
to have such a wonderful
and a beautiful experience...

Wow, mesmerized
by its mystic and magical lure,
once our lips parted,
I wanted more and more.

Under the skies of the solar eclipse,
I was now definitely sure.

Self Imposed

Like quicksand you
engulfed my fiery passion.
The more I struggled to break free
from its grips—my reaction
became more sporadic.

I had no choice but to stay
motionless to its powerful aphrodisiac.
For so long the captor became
ecstasy willingly captive.

The feeling was so intense
and filled with passion.
I could feel the sensation
from head to toe.

Body swirling and shaking violently
and uncontrollably then bam!
I'm in, your moisture explodes—
releasing my inhibitions from the
imprisonment that was long ago self imposed.

Caressing your mind is where
I find the intensity to build our fire.
The words that you speak pierces
my bones and takes me higher.

Beautification

The heights of your greatness
is depicted by the validity of your character.

Within the core lies the basic principles
that makes up your essence.

Your purpose is fueled
by the determination and internal strength
within your soul...

Through perseverance, you'll stand tall
amidst the trials,
tribulations
and adversity of life.

The spiritual, mental, and
physical maturation of being
fortifies your existence.

In the divine scheme of your role
in the continuous process
of beautification of self.

Curiosity

The aura of love is written
all over your beautiful being.

Your energy is my aphrodisiac—
stimulating my soul, and
providing much needed healing.

I, for so long, believed that
loneliness would be my
ultimate destiny and fate...

To have that special and unique someone
who would love me for me!
I knew I had to be very patient and wait.

When I saw you, I felt the intensity
right from the beginning.

You were everything I ever
wanted, desired, and was seeking.
Seeing your smile excited me;
brought me into a natural high.

In this journey of life,
I want you always by my side.
Finding ways to make you happy
will be what I'm thinking of.

Together, we'll expand into
the powerful fulfilling manifestation
of our sensuous, wonderful, beautiful
and enchanted love.

Willing and learning one another;
growing strong in its divine blessings
in full awareness daily and nightly.

To live out our romantic fairytale journey
as with the innocence of children—
in a moment of curiosity.

Tenderness

Waking up next to you
every day and night is definitely
the best highlight of my life.
I was once a ship cruising
along without any direction.
You took the helm and brought
it into a new destination.

Now my soul and being
is in fullness of much exhilaration.
Your smile is the wind that sets
my sail and each mission in love.
It brings such success and happiness
and will always prevail.

You're the beacon of hope that guides me
through the storms and fog of life.
I, out of faith, follow your loving voice,
for you're the bounty…
and the treasure is your love
in which is the ultimate prize.

When we touch I fall further
and more with you, in love.
I love you so much
with all my heart and soul.

Wherever you lead, baby,
I will happily and definitely forsake all
and without hesitation surely go.

You're everything in this world I'll ever need.
Your healthy lovin provides and supplies
my spiritual, mental
and physical being to fullness.

Everyday, we're together,
I'm the most grateful man and so very—
very blessed to truly experience
your awesome tenderness.

Happily Reside

While the stars and moon
share their light with the sky.

I am so happy to have you
here with me, by my side.

Precious moments were made for nights like this.
It's pure ecstasy when you're this close to me.

It's even more special as we both pull close
to one another and gently kiss...

There's no other place I'd rather be
than in your lap of pleasure.

For you are so beautiful and priceless,
like gems of a long lost treasure.

In love, forever, we'll happily reside
for all the days of our lives.

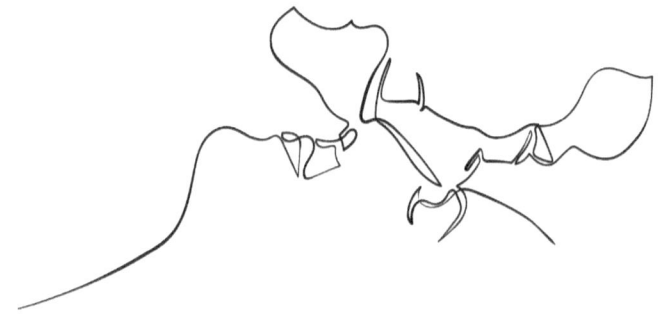

Keep Me Coming

I was just here sitting and reminiscing
about the love we both gratefully share.
I look up to the heavens and smile,
because no other love can truly compare.

I thank God that out of all the wonderful
and beautiful things he has made,
you're the one for me, he has specially delivered
to be a part of my earthly days.

So many souls spend a whole lifetime
searching for a Love to find.
You were so close and nearby, always
right within the sight of my eyes...

I was so intent on instant gratification,
that I almost lost a friendship
and love like yours, filled with happiness
and soul's enlightened passion.

Now it's you that I always dream about and think of.
You fill my mind, body and soul—
so that it overflows.

You, so beautifully, and unconditionally
keep me coming for love.

On Love's Foundations

My eyes are so blessed
to have seen your uniqueness.
From the moment I laid my eyes on you.
I knew it was too good to be true.

Everything I ever dreamt of—
majestically wrapped in the essence of love.
Every night I pray for strength...
As for you, I will not lose hope as I patiently wait.

Now all of a sudden, like a powerful rush,
you appeared as my one and only lovely soulmate.

Now loneliness is no more—
as together we both begin a new chapter
in our romance and prepare
to walk through its inviting door.

You're my beloved Queen, keeper of my heart,
object of my desires and fantasies;
both in reality and my dreams...

Together, we'll walk hand in hand
facing life's storms and adversities,
on love's beautiful and powerful foundations,
we will forever triumphantly stand.

Come True

No other can take away my heartache, hurt and pain.
Your smile and soft tender touch can heal my broken
heart and make me feel whole once again.

When God made you, he definitely broke the mold.
To have you forever here on earth in my life, I'm willing
to go through the fire and even sell my soul.

Your love is so deliciously good and plenty, and to find
you, my precious jewel, I had to go through many.
It was worth the long traveled and painstaking search.

Now, up in your sweetness...

I lay so snuggled and comfortably in its loving worth.
You're so very beautiful and amazing, that you're very
admired and adored.

To be the blessed recipient to receive this special and
unique gift, it warms my heart and soul to its very core.
I thank God for thinking of me when he made you.

I love and appreciate you, so that even if it takes me
a lifetime… I'll make all your dreams and
fantasies come true.

Pleasing you is the desire of my heart.
Your kiss is where passion starts.

Endlessly

You came unto me...
Like a sudden rush of fresh air
or a soft cool summer breeze.
I was caught off guard
and immediately fell to my knees.

Where did this come from
so swiftly, and why?
All I knew…
right from that moment, my soul felt
so greatly reinvigorated, so alive!

You were everything I had always
dreamed of and so much more.
When I first laid my eyes on you,
there was no doubt that you
were destined for me, in this world.

I was 100% sure...
This union was custom made for
two from the heavens above.
I for you and you for me—showered forever
with unconditional blessings and love.

I, together with the birds,
come up daily with a brand new,
beautiful and inspirational tune.
To celebrate your beauty, strength,
grace, virtue and perseverance
time and time again...

Words can't truly capture
how much you really mean to me.
So I compose this song
from my heart and soul,
to immortalize you forever
in my dreams and reality.

To celebrate you—
lifting you on high.
For bringing much needed,
life-sustaining love and happiness
to that in me which is inside.

In total peace and harmony,
I rely and rest in you so confidently,
protectively and comfortably.

I for you and you for me—
loving one another so gently and endlessly.

Love Will Always Last

When I first laid my eyes on you,
I knew right then and there
that love finally came to pay its dues.

It sent my mind into a magical whirlwind
causing my life to never be the same.

I tried to deny it,
even tried to fight it...
but when I was around you,
all I could see was that I couldn't hide it.

We wanted each other
and truly everyone could tell.
A love like ours sure would grow
and as lovers we really could excel.

Oh baby,
how I would have given anything
just to hold you forever close in my arms.
To be there always whenever you need me
and protect you from pain and harm.

Yes, it's true that love came quick and fast
but now with you in my arms, with me,
love will always last.

Love My Way

Let me love my way into your heart
so that I'll always be there.

Let me love my way into your heart
so that you'll know that I care.

Love will blossom within its time,
this I know.

Let's become entangled in its heavenly bind
that will never let us both go.

This, what I'm saying, is just a start...
Good times are ahead for us.

Sweetheart, if you let me love my way
into your heart.

More Beautiful

There's nothing more beautiful
than true love unfurled.
Yes, a love that's experienced
between a boy and girl.

To be strengthened everyday,
as life goes through the perils of time...

Yes, a love that's complex
and complicated as the human mind.
Baby, the love that we have—
goes way, way beyond comprehension.

Everyday, I'm drawn into you
by a very strong connection.

Yes, this is a love blessed from above
and when it's poured on, I can't get enough.
Yes, now looking back through all the
memories that love has put us through.

I can agree,
there's nothing more beautiful
in this world as you…

Love's Infinite Fountain

I look for your love to help me
make it through the day and to show me the way.

I'm the seed, and your love is the sun,
water, and all the nutrients I need to
spiritually, mentally, and physically grow.

In my life, you will always stay by my side.
I enjoy making sweet, slow,
and tender love to you—day or night.

It puts me on such a natural high.
I'm floating on the clouds, or even air.
When I look deep into your truly mesmerizing
and hypnotic eyes, whisper I love you—
it's from my heart and soul, and very sincere.

Together, we can make it
to the top of the mountain.

In you, I humbly and graciously drink
of your essence of wholeness from your
soul-quenching kiss and love's infinite fountain.

Love is living water
which keeps our roots healthy to grow.
Without you, is something I wouldn't
ever want to know.

Honey Nectar

In the garden of exotic fruits...
I was in total delight at so many delicious
and tasty treats and sights.

Yes, I tried so many
but I wasn't quite satisfied
The more I indulged,
the more empty I felt inside.

I was just going through the motions
until one day, out of nowhere...
I accidentally stumbled upon your
sweet and sticky potion.
One taste, and I knew—
it was truly meant for me.

Immediately, its powerful and
calming collaboration of nutrition and
sweetness flowed throughout my soul.
Now, I'm the most blessed.

Yes, by far...
To be the one and only to taste
and experience the joys of savoring
rawness and the purity of your honey nectar.

Captured by your smile—delighted with your kiss.
Your love, is the comfort that I feel
deep within my spirit.

Moon

Meet me on the moon
so I can spread the remnants
of my star-studded body all over you.

Gently glaze my lovin'
all over your enchanted grounds.
And watch as our seeds naturally sprout
manifestations of a love of labor unbound.

The constellations of the mystical stars
and planets will shine our path
with their divine beauty.

Humanity will look up in the skies,
willing to be inspired and delighted to
majestically behold our love's glory.

Our oneness will transcend
through the portal of time.
It will stimulate and transform the
body, mind, and soul to intertwine.

I long to know what makes you glow,
on your amazing and voluptuous landscape.
In your essence so deep on the moon,
is where every new dawn I want to wake.

In Tune

When I look deeply
Into your dreamy eyes,
I am totally exposed.

I can see the true you
Beautiful core of your aura
And a precious soul.

You inject me with your
Powerful potency of lovin'
Which in my veins freely flows.

The exuberance that it sows
And manifests, now has me
In a much simpler and happier
Tune that I blissfully sing.

The birds are in awe
As I dance daily
In tune with them all

Singing the sensuous
Melodic lyrics
True compositions
Of lovin' you bring.

My Favorite Things

I'm on a natural high
When I suddenly and deeply
Stare into your very
Alluring and beautiful eyes.

My passions start to overflow
As my anticipation for kissing
Your sweet tender lips
Excitedly grows and grows.

I can sit and watch you
All throughout my earthly days.

When I'm feeling out of sync,
To make me feel better,
You know what to do
And the exact words to say.

Together we'll go on a romantic journey
Of our love's sensuous synchronization
Of our soul's awakening.

We sit at the table of pleasure
And immerse ourselves
In its enchanting partaking.

We are very blissfully happy
And join the birds daily
In the exuberant melodic songs we sing.

This, and unconditionally,
I lovin you and you lovin me
Are among pursuing our great romance
And a few of my favorite things.

Shower Me

Your sensuous meteorological showers
replenish me.

Your divine moisturizer
is my soul replenisher.

I take handfuls and drench my body
from head to toe,
I am revitalized anew.

My tools of essential oils
spread easily...
across your majestic contour,
and landscapes of stimulating and powerful
identification of your womanhood.

The dripping of its nutrients
manifests shadows of your core being
on the earth's grounds.

I swim into the unconscious boundaries naked
experiencing the highest compliment,
of expression through ecstasy.

Enticing Grips

We glide towards one another
so effortlessly—
We slowly wrap our arms
around each other's waist;
our eager lips, yearning to taste.

When our lips finally do meet…

It's pure pleasure and ecstasy.
Under your powerful lure and spell,
so deeply I anxiously—head first
with my heart on my sleeve, fell.

I can't think of anyone else
but only you—it's you.
I'm always in a love trance,
unable to remember the things
I either say or do.

Truth be told...

The more I try to climb
out from its depths—
the deeper I get.
I continue to slip further
into its enticing grips.

My feet are planted deeply in fertile ground
and rooted in your love.

Natural Beauty

I exposed my inner inhibitions
to you so completely.

My passions
run through my existence so freely
and vehemently.

I am weak from its exotic
stirring of my soul...
I'm holding on as tight as I can
and I refuse to let it go.

You're so very beautiful
and all I want and need.

I'm so very happy
and blessed to share,
the same air you breathe.

It's pure, tantalizing and mesmerizing.
Toe tingling experience,
of ecstasy.

My essence is poured
into your calm waters of pleasure.

We become one powerful expression
of erotic artistry—
Arousing the sensory stimulation
of its raw and divine natural beauty.

Do you want me?

Yes
I can taste you
I'll run my essence through your hair;
make all your anxiety disappear.
Run my fingertips gently across your
contours of pure loveliness.

I'll replace happiness in the place of fear.
My tastebuds will delight to relish in
your sweetness.

Our lust for love and life will shine
like beautiful jewels...
Your kiss will be my replenishing tool.

In our relevance we will enjoy
the elegance of this powerful
and sensuous romance.

I Want You

Telepathy

In the fields of pleasure and ecstasy.
I live to the fullest my most beautiful
and powerful desires and fantasies.

In your arms I find my rapture and
I'm enraptured by your sweet elixir.
In my mind and heart, you have
become a stable fixture—

I love you unconditionally and our love
knows no boundaries and has no limits.
Into the universe, we both bind and
synchronize and truly transcend.

We are as one soul,
being telepathy and our desires.
Manifesting them through the
cascading stream of free flowing
unconscious with freedom of expression.

Sleeping Beauty

In the still of the night
I lay beside you and
watch you as you sleep.
There are no words to
express a love this deep.

In-between the sheets is
where our oneness meets.
Quietly at peace we lay
as morning brings a new
and enlightened day.

Loving you is the purpose
of my soul and I'll always
be loyal—come what may.

In heavenly glory
is where our powerful love
will forever stay.

Your love is the fertilizer that sprouts
a harvest of tantalizing fruit.

Mastered

I was one who never
believed in fairy tales or
if they even came true.

My fairy tale was manifested
into fruition when my eyes
had a chance to behold you.

Now my whole perception
of life and love has drastically
changed so very much.

Now the radiant sunshine
has replaced the dreary dark clouds.
There's no more rain as I yearn
to hold, kiss, and feel your tender touch.

I love you with all my soul and might.
In your lair of pure honey,
I find my pleasure
and tantalizing delights.

We'll go away…
to a distant enchanted land.
Where all our dreams are reality
and love is in full demand.

There together and forever,
we'll live out our romantic life
in happiness ever after.

When it's all said and done...
Spiritually, mentally, and physically;
our love will be known and mastered.

Dreams Are Made Of

I dream about you every single night
wishing you were here.

Entwined in each other's mind
as I dream your lips are kissing mine.
Our hearts beat in rhythm,
like your voice echoing thru time.

Our love is strong
like an atomic bomb!
From my head to my toes,
my love for you just grows
stronger and flows.

Many nights of happy endings...
Holding you and squeezing you tight.
The comfort of your presence is always
greatly satisfying and feels so right.

If dreams were a reality
and every fantasy came true.
I would spend my time in
this hot steamy fairytale with you.

Where you can always
be my knight and shining armor,
I'll be your princess too.
Making love on a rainbow
in ecstasy with you.

Between two destined lovers
we'll inspire a long line of others
in the passion of their dreams—

Because this is...
what dreams are made of.

Reside

I love holding your body close to mine
amidst the candles which burn slowly
all throughout the magical night.

Two hearts beating—
coming together as one is where our love
has fully prospered and begun…

There's no other love I want here with me.
In my kingdom, you're my beloved Queen.

We'll rewrite the blueprint for love and
give humanity a new heavenly alignment.
Something so lucidly magnificent, majestical,
amazing, and breathtakingly original.

In paradise, it'll always be you and I.
Where we are, there's love, happiness,
joy and contentment will also reside.

Your gentleness is the reason
our love grows stronger.

The Love Game

When we hug and kiss
We are participating
In the love game.

We're both so immersed in it,
Our hearts are victoriously
And ecstatically happy...
More and more as we
Constantly play.

I love it a lot when we play
Our love game.

I fully take advantage
Of the opportunity
To get to know you
So much better.

We can play it no matter
What the weather.

We don't need any other
Players or participants
In our world.

We started out slow
But after some time,
We began to grow
As we watched our love
Strengthened and unfurled.

This is one game
That never gets old.

It's so invigorating
Stimulating and mesmerizing
To our existence and essence
Of our divine souls.

Happy and fulfilled are my days
As we continue looking forward
To play the Love game.

Living, Breathing, and Being

As I throw my whole essence
into your fiery furnace
of insatiable appetite.

It burns like the raging passions
that flow like the natural wonders
of the divine earth.

The internal heat boils my ecstasy
to full radiance and solidifies
our value and worth.

I want you badly and seriously
as I crave for it.
My love erupts and comes down while
at its most anticipated mystical peak.

Your candy kisses drive me
so delirious then I get so weak.
Its sugary flavor comes in my
favorite color and a tasty treat.

Mixed with our natural fluids
that run freely from our beautiful
intertwined vessels of needing.

It's not only erotic and exotic
but highly explosive like T.N.T.

We come together arising and expanding
perfect and unconscious completion—
deeply layered in love's secretion.

Laying next to one another
is the most powerful and amazing part
of living, breathing, and being.

The Busy Bee

In the fields
of passionate delights,
I am drawn to your sweet sticky lovin'
like a busy bee around it—
I'll be happily buzzin.

The lingering aroma has a
very alluring, tempting, and
stimulating scent to it.

I, the busy bee, long to pollinate
and complete your existence,
bringing it to beauty's expression
in full bloom…

The flowers and fruits manifested
from our combination of the
mixture of divine beings,
brings a nostalgic feeling of
raw instinctive completeness.

Galactic Love

The depths of my heart
pours poetry as I pick up my pen.
Dreaming my lover is dancing
on top of the moon with me.

Embracing my inner peace,
Our love illuminates the stars and
passion takes us beyond mars;
wrapped in the gentleness of your arms.

Pleasure is vast like the galaxy...
Our lips are a place of how
much your touch matters to me.
The milky way is my reality.

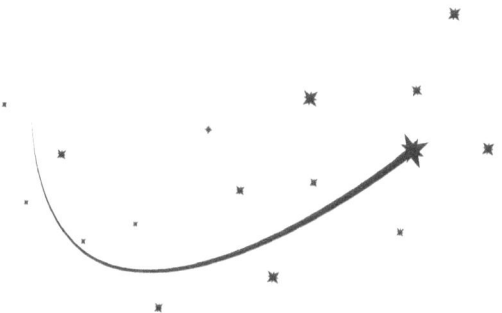

The navigation system of my heart
led me to you.

www.ingramcontent.com/pod-product-compliance
Lightning Source LLC
Chambersburg PA
CBHW031300290426
44109CB00012B/661